Collins

easy learning

Reading and rhyme

Ages 3–5

fox

box

Carol Medcalf

How to use this book

- Find a quiet, comfortable place to work, away from distractions.
- This book has been written in a logical order, so start at the first page and work your way through.
- Help with reading the instructions where necessary and ensure that your child understands what to do.
- This book is a gentle introduction to reading and rhyme, starting with rhyming pictures and progressing to rhyming words. Help your child to sound out the rhyming sounds as you work through the book together. This will help them to hear the rhymes more clearly. Try to share many more rhymes and stories with your child to complement the activities in this book.
- If an activity is too difficult for your child then do more of our suggested practical activities (see Activity note) and return to the page when you know that they're likely to achieve it.
- Always end each activity before your child gets tired so that they will be eager to return next time.
- Help and encourage your child to check their own answers as they complete each activity.
- Let your child return to their favourite pages once they have been completed. Talk about the activities they enjoyed and what they have learnt.

Special features of this book:

- **Activity note:** situated at the bottom of every left-hand page, this suggests further activities and encourages discussion about what your child has learnt.
- **Nursery rhyme panel:** situated at the bottom of every right-hand page, this contains picture prompts and the first rhyming lines of well-known nursery rhymes. Say the rhymes together, emphasising the words in red. These can be sung wherever you are and provide great practice of rhyming words. Younger children will be able to use the picture prompts to remember the rhyme; older children may be able to read the text.
- **Certificate:** the certificate on page 24 should be used to reward your child for their effort and achievement. Remember to give your child plenty of praise and encouragement, regardless of how they do.

Published by Collins
An imprint of HarperCollins*Publishers* Ltd
The News Building
1 London Bridge Street
London
SE1 9GF

Browse the complete Collins catalogue at
www.collins.co.uk

© HarperCollins*Publishers* Ltd 2006
This edition © HarperCollins*Publishers* Ltd 2015
12
ISBN 978-0-00-815156-0

The author asserts the moral right to be identified as the author of this work.

All rights reserved. No part of this publication may be reproduced, stored in a retrieval system, or transmitted, in any form or by any means, electronic, mechanical, photocopying, recording or otherwise, without the prior permission of Collins.

British Library Cataloguing in Publication Data
A Catalogue record for this publication is available from the British Library.
Written by Carol Medcalf

Design and layout by Lodestone Publishing Limited and Contentra Technologies Ltd
Illustrated by Jenny Tulip
Cover design by Sarah Duxbury and Paul Oates
Cover illustration by John Haslam
Project managed by Sonia Dawkins

Printed in Great Britain by Bell and Bain Ltd, Glasgow

MIX
Paper from responsible source
FSC™ C007454

This book is produced from independently certified FSC™ paper to ensure responsible forest management.

For more information visit:
www.harpercollins.co.uk/green

Contents

How to use this book	2
Odd one out	4
Spot the difference	5
Rhyming pictures	6
Odd one out	7
Story time	8
2-letter words	9
Rhyming pairs	10
More rhymes	11
Story time	12
Which word?	13
Vowels	14
Odd one out	16
Story time	17
Picture match	18
Hidden words	19
Find the letters	20
Yes or no?	21
Rhyming words	22
Reading practice	23
Certificate	24
Answers	Inside back cover

Odd one out

- Draw a circle round the picture that is different in each row.

Spot the difference

- There are 5 differences between these two pictures. Can you find them?

Hickory dickory dock
The mouse ran up the clock

Rhyming pictures

- Draw a (circle) round the two pictures that rhyme in each row.

Make up silly rhymes together: "My name's boo and I live in the zoo." Sometimes get it wrong: "My name's Holly and I've got a……(leave a pause while they may guess the right rhyme) banana,… no…My name's Holly and I've got a lolly".

Odd one out

- Cross out the picture that does not rhyme in each set.

Little Miss **Muffet**
Sat on a **tuffet**

Story time

- Look at the pictures and tell the story.

Reading stories together is the perfect way to start your child on the right path to reading and to develop their love of books. On this page you may need to give your child prompts to tell the story and discuss what is happening. Say: 'I wonder what they are doing?'

2-letter words

- Cross out the word that is different in each row.

it	it	it	at	it
am	am	an	am	am
on	or	on	on	on
us	up	up	up	up
if	if	if	in	if

Jack and Jill
Went up the hill

Rhyming pairs

- Do the pairs in each row rhyme? Yes (✓) or no (✗)?

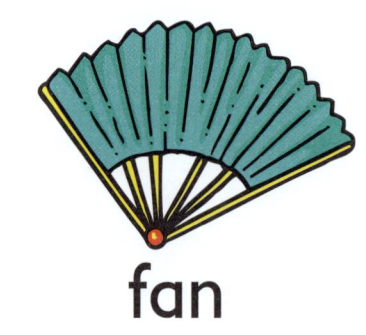

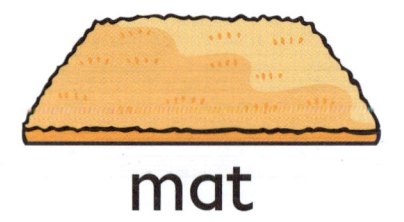

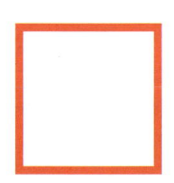

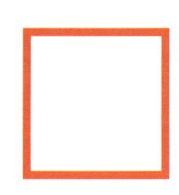

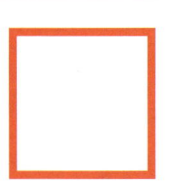

van	fan	✓
tap	mat	☐
car	cup	☐
fish	dish	☐
cake	ball	☐

Practice making up rhymes together. Don't worry if your child doesn't understand at first, they will gradually. Try to use examples from this book and then think of your own together.

More rhymes

- Look at the picture and finish the rhyme. Draw a (circle) round the correct word.

The cat sat on the

bed
mat

The fox jumped on the

box
bowl

The cat chased the

rat
hen

The ball is on the

table
wall

Incy Wincy spider climbed up the spout
Down came the rain and washed the spider out

Story time

- Look at the pictures and tell the story. What do you think happens next?

Help your child to understand that you read a book from front to back, the pages from left to right, top to bottom and that print conveys meaning.

Which word?

- Draw lines to match the words to the pictures.

bus
cat ———
car

tin
pot
dog

bag
cot
bug

win
box
sun

six
zip
bin

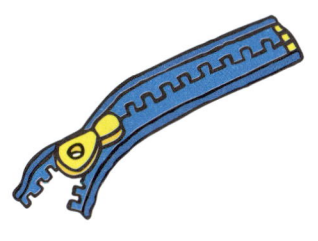

See-saw, Margery Daw

Vowels

- Fill in the missing middle letters. Read the words.

write **a**   c a t   b __ t   r __ t

write **e**   h __ n   b __ d   r __ d

write **i**   p __ n   b __ n   z __ p

write **o**   d __ g   m __ p   c __ t

write **u**   j __ g   c __ p   b __ s

For this activity, help your child to sound out the 'a' sound and then hear it in the three words. Think of other words together that contain the 'a' sound. Repeat for e, i, o and u sounds.

- Say the word for each picture. Draw a (circle) round the middle sound.

a   e   i   o   u

a   e   i   o   u

a   e   i   o   u

a   e   i   o   u

a   e   i   o   u

Old Mother Hubbard
Went to the cupboard

Odd one out

- Cross out the word that is different in each row.

cat	cat	cat	cup
bin	bin	bug	bin
red	bed	bed	bed
dog	dig	dog	dog
jet	jet	let	jet

- Write these words. They are all written above to help you.

_ _ _   _ _ _   _ _ _   _ _ _

This activity helps children to look closely at words and see subtle differences. By saying the letter sounds individually, they should be able to read all these words.

16

Story time

- Look at the pictures and tell the story.

Twinkle twinkle little star
How I wonder what you are!

Picture match

- Draw lines to match the pictures and the words.

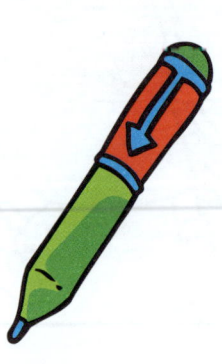

cap   bag
can   bug
cut   bib

web   tap
win   tag
wet   ten

pan   box
pen   bad
pip   bog

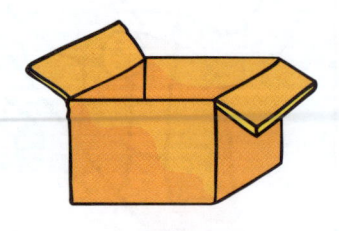

Look at the pictures above and then sound out each of the three choices. Ask your child which one is the right word.

Hidden words

- Find these words that are hidden in the grid below.

man   red   pin   cot   cup

m	a	n	f	l
y	z	r	e	d
s	p	i	n	q
c	o	t	r	m
h	l	c	u	p

- Draw lines to match the words to the pictures.

pin   van   sit
pop   vet   sip
pip   vap   six

Wee Willie Winkie runs through the town
Upstairs and downstairs in his nightgown

19

Find the letters

- Look at the pictures in each row. Colour the boxes with the correct letters to make the word.

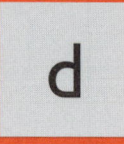

| d | j | k | o | g |

| m | c | a | w | t |

| h | o | e | n | g |

| q | f | o | h | x |

Make up silly tongue twisters together, using the same letter for the start of each word: "Marcus made Millie munchie, mauve marshmallows" and "Thomas tried to tackle the tired, tearful tiger".

Yes or no?

- Look at each picture. Does the word underneath match the picture? Yes (✔) or no (✘)?

jug

dog

hat

log

bin

zip

It's raining, it's pouring
The old man is snoring

Rhyming words

- Draw a (circle) round the two words that rhyme in each row.

wet	dog	vet	dot
fog	dad	log	hat
mug	jug	can	bib
pip	pet	sip	hid
fun	job	rug	run
bun	leg	peg	hot

The words on page 23 are high frequency words that often appear in stories. They are amongst the first words that children learn when reading.

Reading practice

- Look at the pictures and fill in the missing words. Read the sentences.

Mum   Dad   dog   cat

This is ___ ___ ___ .

This is ___ ___ ___ .

This is a ___ ___ ___ .

This is a ___ ___ ___ .

They are all going to play!

Humpty Dumpty sat on the wall
Humpty Dumpty had a great fall!

23

Well done .... (name)

You have finished!

Now you know how to read and rhyme!

Age .... Date ....